«Pro(m)bois(e)»

Thibault Raoult

Opo Books & Objects
abadpennyreview.com

«Pro(m)bois(e)»
Copyright ©2016 by Thibault Raoult
ISBN-10: 0-9973048-0-4
ISBN-13: 978-0-9973048-0-0
Library of Congress Control Number: 2016903458

Cover design by Johnny Damm

Marcelle & Jean
VIVE LA NORMANDIE

A: *rhymes with* FRAMBOISE

B: *here! let* (M)(E) *say that*

der
some
thun

[IC]
dialog

some

some

thing

to have on

Quail Sea Situs

Pro-you-know-who is stranded on Etna, who is an island. He suffers there because of his role in F=I=R=E.

Etna keeps Pro near and dear to her by means of a molten BROW, *whose* TRAFFIC *examines Pro's organs each and every day.*

Meanwhile, o'er QUAIL SEA *is Echo—that vehicle of rumor/soft journalism. She overlaps on occasion with 4Winds.*

In this BEIGE-BAY: <u>*deference happens*</u>.

[Horizon: <u>Lotte</u>.]

Etna stacks sun on Pro

Until he silences
His holy game of

Slug/subjunctive

Pro pisses on his chains and watches colors come out.

[BEIGE-BAY ACTIVITAY:] Echo alights whenever Etna says hello.

When brought together, their bangs double, take available waters.

How's that, 4Winds?

Echo coughs. People glisten.

The logistics of dream-space fry.

And   light   like   that

[be]—Tombpupil.

BEIGE-BAY's got

An open face

Hit da yolk
Bees be released

Hospi-TOTALITY

After *any* two days in Etna's TRAFFIC

Pro's inna[te] slush

Approaches a
Feathered cry

Pro's got a PINK SAUCE: QUESTION

Etna's BROW does one thing

Echo's Croakiris another

Pro believes: clearing is relative:

And index to relative: Etna's bangs

Sound sweet: in the after

Echo blows lemongrass down into BEIGE-BAY

Cooling Pro who welcomes her any idea

Echo each etch
We cannot be

Voila

ci

ta-ta

ta

Nobody reads a room like Echo, who

In her biop-hoverin' o'er QUAIL SEA

(occasional puncture to glide on and on [anon])

Suggests a Top, enacts a Tap

And fans [*grunt*] (M)(E)

The Dry Sometimes.

Pro has feelings for skeins too.

There's always Tombpupil.

And Chopang. Sour Chopang.

(see: Chopin)

Pro perforated wakes and feels around for so-called nâcre.

Anticipates another HOT CAKE:

Always a sign of Etna's

Hospitotality

you shouldn't have

Pro:

Since Kossof's got my back [*looks around*]
I must confess I love Echo's NODES.

Echo's too legible to quit [*partially sung*]
Too legible to use silencers.

Echo:

Never did get what others did mean by *seasoning* / (M)(E).

Etna:

One learns so much from how another's shadow guzzles ghazals.

I'm speaking of Pro, who each day resembles more and more a GOAT UND PUDDLE:

My HOT CAKES to thank for this.

Pro:

The first five months weren't so bad.

Then I realized it wasn't an audition.

And island lavender

Squeals:

How Echo harnesses Etna
(as Etna sleeps)

How Echo uses Etna's TRAFFIC
To tamper w/ Pro's chains

As 4Winds curdle Etna's BROW

[Echo-cutive order]

One osier one crawls in Pro's ear

And helps him hear BEIGE-BAY ACTIVITAY

And so Pro escapes on osier, floating off

Under my bed

<u>The sky</u>

Pro:

Etna maybe you been ADEN ALAR
This entire   salty   mostly
Spurious time   all of time

A nuptial presence   a half-sung
Hymn in a field   below
A goddess   in a field

her helmet dawn
her bite alembic

We do not live in enlightened AEG.

We do not live with space / as emotion

As Echo / starts (M)(E) toward spare sun.

Cadeau De La Mort:

Pro Was Here

Tide saw through (M)(E) but
Tide saw (M)(E) through

New Boise Situs

Sweet* Lotte has left a continent behind to participate in a New Boise production of PAS DE PEPINS: the opera.

Sandy Bison Lovebird knows about the QUAIL SEA situs, knows even more about New Boise; he sponsors an erotic BOIS—a terrain of TREENAGE HYMNS—far from both, across a WARM PLAIN, past mountainous HEEL, and through a PASS monitored by Boar, whose wren-like offspring—though a handful—are a delight.

Sandy gets Lotte's consent in New Boise, and they make for WARM PLAIN.

*[Shakespearean filler]

Wherever it is she's from, Lotte loves squats.

Which is GAE, real light.

Sandy Bison Lovebird meditates ofTen.

He frequently wins——

XaXaXa [*Russian laughter*].

Sometimes he calls his meditation THE BRONZE RUSH.

The Bison Lovebird waits up for Lotte, but Sandy plays down alembic in their upper bodies.

Oh, the rush as BRONZE approaches.

Stepping in chalk in downtown New Boise

And then wandering off, Sandy

Accidentally articulates his era.

Lotte:

World begins lightheartedly

What I want when I want birds

(a) bolt through (a) spring

Lotte:

People used to kill for Sandy's tracks.
I was never one.

I touched two stones.
I kept them apart.

(dissolve all
(clerical
(padding

In sincerest New Boise Sandy habitually

Runs out of context

Mid-bite

And ADEN ALAR hints

Maybe this is what dogs do

Lotte:

An origin of language: two stones

Coming together

In the interest of will-call leaves

I'll settle for cobalt curtsy

By the end of PAS DE PEPINS everything's been given to us. In stone.

When you see Lotte scramble—you should know where to put everything.

Lotte *prefers* protracted
Glow and—not gossamer—
Her stage allows
Low hum, custody
Of which Sandy
Mocks with wax.

Sandy sleeps and asks for hame that Lotte might've left behind when she came completely to New Boise.

That's no way for Lovebird to behave!

[Lotte posits: beneath Sandy's wing: more wing.]

Lotte:

Lovebird gave (M)(E) whiplash

Whiplash gave (M)(E) tide

Sandy Bison Lovebird

's slow <u>stone</u> yclept

a slow <u>stone</u>

Lotte's nerves: worth knowing

Un-American Sandy Bison Lovebird

Sleeps in a bonnet.

His spiffy hoof (frontleft) can render negligees.

The Bison Lovebird believes he already thanked (M)(E) thoroughly

For foreign thorns, and goes at my romance with pliers.

Why, he has pliers. Why he has pliers.

<u>Nekton</u> <u>Nekton</u> he's our be(a)st. [*chanted*]

Lotte:

I'm losing it, the brains behind glass.

4Winds be less / perverse these days, owing to what New Boise's sheriffs found under their pillows under their damp nightingales.

Could have been thorns. Could have been pliers.
Could have been foreign. Could have been (M)(E).

WILL TREBLE FOR TREEN

WILL BUCKLE FOR MOLT

WILL TALLY FOR SHOOK-OUT TWIN

[*partially sung*]

:

how Sandy Bison Lovebird distills his dream of pedaling toy tractors to buy éclairs with his favorite rapper.

Sandy drapes his body over New Boise, loving it and loving that New Boise ain't Dieppe 'cause that means Sandy can have both New Boise <u>and</u> Dieppe in his life.

*Lotte, unlock
my detergent*

What Lotte knows
Slides up thru Sandy
The Bison Lovebird

Who only deals in
Beige. Beige
Symmetries?

As Lotte and Sandy's collective pubis—what stammel locks!—crosses WARM PLAIN, it definitively notices 4Winds are tired of keeping "very us" fire [the] alive.

Tempered landscapes

When I write in French
There is no traffic,
Love.

Rewind Situs

For Pro to survive Etna he must keep near all plausible throats.

Pro's shadow sweats soundly as Pro bounces off the felt time. Pro beams as Echo brings him sound / Lotte's thinking.

Banal Pro's Dead. New Pro Widens.

Echo → *Pro:*

Be loud around others' ideas of flame.

Pro loves to leak

But if he asks Etna for mercy she says:

Never was time or tongue for this [*chanted*]

(M)(E)

I love to leak

No, never was time or tongue.

Pro's days shape others' tongues

while Etna guesses at birds (likely puffins)
while Echo corrects negatives
while Pro supplies organs

4Winds
e'er frank
lather up GOAT UND PUDDLE

4*WINDS:*

Today we praise Etna's GELatinous impulse

Her instinct for the pudding of others' sublimated desires

All without moving a muscle

Psychic Pickle [Pro turns inside out]

Pro:

In the course of selling water filters vicariously, I learned I was SCHERZO——

What Echo and the rest had been telling (M)(E) for years.

It only strengthened my resolve to wear ONE GLOVE.

Etna:

I taught I saw waters near Pro rewind.

Echo:

4Winds don't care what you think.

They care how you move.

Hunh Echo?
Lo mismo?

Like notches into cherry wood 4Winds

Carve antithesis into Etna's BROW.

Admission two kumquats.

Pro:

Oh Etna,

You shouldn't have to hammer out my shadow like this.

Whatever *we* have——
Ours is visual.

Pro makes a relish of shadow, then a brief statement:

What is called belly
What is called boating
What is called both

4Winds:

In Etna's and Echo's moods we disclose dreams

(dreams natural and obedient to OS)

And our concepts, too, of BEIGE-BAY and osier.

Should Sandy reach BOIS intact, our relatives speaking, we'll know (finally):

Each leaf be Sandy's eye.

And Lotte, deliver! my part in PAS DE PEPINS
In a clastic AVE.

What might be sung before the end.

(Pro's trulyf Open End)

FLAVOID FLAVOID

IT-NO-GA(M)(E)!?

GO|WIT|GA

It's all the same song, Pro says.

I say—

It's all the same song.

Rose asp beneath Pro's tongue adds hum to Etna's BROW like butte does ooze through Sandy Bison Lovebird's okay saddle.

And, hoping to siphon eventually what Lotte used on stage during PAS DE PEPINS: the oper-perdu-ah, Lotte's ancestors ask openly:

Dear Unit Above, will there be a time when Sandy Bison Lovebird and Lotte are not fully accessible?

Fus(ion)elage: Sandy's Tat

Pro knows about BOIS.

Far from okay, Pro hopes to join Sandy and Lotte there one day.

WHATEVER. WE LIVE ON DEW.

Reading backwards, we can know what Sandy Bison Lovebird thinks.

Moss has been published for our benefit, Lotte. Lots.

If there's one thing Echo expects in Etna it's stout.

When two worlds flare in a stranger

They say fossils will take over New Boise,

Assume anything.

PAS DE PEPINS

Marsyas believes he'd love *paille* even more acutely. Riata Largo, lavender loves a girl/light who knocks stain-glass right out of its holster.

Pro—toothless wet—starts his life over in sincerest New Boise.

S<small>ANCERRE</small>

<small>FOR THE</small>

<small>ALL-AGES</small>

BEIGE-BAY loves the glare Echo gathers off Etna.

What would a jasmine and dragonfly epidemic look like anyway?

We musk ask for we losk our voice in Pierre De Ronsards.

C'est tout jus(te).

Pro:

Etna's kilns can compute
To master mint / (M)(E)
For all I care

Ideas are <u>discrete</u> or *would be*

Had Sandy Bison Lovebird ever known how to order or how to put on his own saddle and tie Lotte's boots.

You know what they say: any UTOPIA a bit crowded makes for GROUP TOOTH.

How you say *blood*   inhabits
(how you blood the both)

Saddle unbound
Saddle not bound

For Sandy Bison Lovebird——
Increasingly into <u>UNBUILT STABLE</u>,

His <u>UNSTABLE</u>.

Echo:

(Am Un
(Anon
(Ano
(Ammun (Enum

[*sung*]

Echo (jealous) makes it so Sandy and Lotte's words fall to the ground. And so they no longer co-evolve.

THE CLEAN HISTORY OF SAYING

TWO THINGS AT ONCE

Helps Lotte (over time) remove Sandy's masks[1]
But can't do a thing for Pro.

---

[1] These are the metaphysical calisthenics of our lives.
                            (light (verse
                            (hearse (at first sight

Vigilance of the Ordinary

[11:32 a.m.] How little sense can you make, Lotte asks (taking in WARM PLAIN around her), will PASS do away with while negating "very us" question? And Sandy answers: paper work—Ooo—papal wok.

Sandy:

Lotte pays (M)(E)

In mouthfuls
Of rosin

And thimbleful
Of <u>late</u>

Lotte:

Europe's just pissed it didn't think of *ketchup* first. In that way.

Lotte:

How empty are your hooves?

Sandy:

I'm infinitely yours to blend.

Lotte:

A sentence is a minor miracle.
Burns but doesn't *burn* burn.
Kneels, doesn't see shapes.
And coupons arrive in time
For us to continue.

Would much prefer palms sometimes, Sandy says, trying to pray w/ hooves.

Lotte:

It's dark now, Sandy.

Shall I bounce off a coupon for you?

Sandy:

WANNA GIVE (M)(E) LIPO, LOTTE,
WITH YOUR TEETH?

We made it to PASS.
Now I need an hour or two to change.

What gives Boar—
identity [clear]
as hotdog soup—
the right to lift us
from our dark?

Boar, come out wherever you are.

In PASS they ask what word for *heaven* is. But when Boar's kids—those beasts of dew—say HERE, Sandy and Lotte turn and continue on to BOIS, of which Sandy has not stopped speaking (in one way or another) since Lotte mounted him in New Boise.

Boar:

To (M)(E) there is no voice that does not bake mud into Rodin.

To (M)(E) there is no voice.

When first Boar's kids did lose their vox tissu

They clawed the earth
And kept their names this way

And soon the birds, at least, were sleeping
With number(s)——

SANDY'S UN-MISSIVES TO LOTTE

Situs: Sandy moves Lotte across WARM PLAIN *and beyond. Sandy gathers nettles as nettles gather Sandy Bison Lovebird.*

§

What light, Lotte, in Schelde II's lap. And what light, Lotte, as dancers drown in pool by Alechinsky. Your dancers know, Rodin, my other hundred mothertongues dissolve near moss? Your dancers know nettles touch me out of dwelling? Your dancers, Rodin, know anything!?

§

What's it take for a Bison to convince you, Lotte, there's no shame? Been meaning to ask: do you read Michaux mostly in mornings? Could just look over, but that's not as much fun as trickling [ditmas] in your direction. What are your feelings about never seeing Schelde II again? Whatever we come across after PASS should offer lap to rival Schelde II's lap. Rodin is rumored to have gone through PASS after Egypt cancelled his mud order. Telecommand me,

§

What bargains on sliders out here in the Open, Lotte, n'est-ce pas? Do apologize for that bumpy stretch back there near desiccated ferns— INTENSE. It was pretty dark and I hadn't had any nettles in a while—my joints were barely functioning. But I made a graph in the dust, let the Open digest its argument, and when you saw the Open's party favor, you brought out the nettles I most enjoy, which really got us moving. Before long we'll hit HEEL, and then shoot straight up to PASS, annexing syllables along the way, preparing for Boar with our incandescent dust-duet.

§

Our tight own winds do undo buttes we streak by on WARM PLAIN, Lotte. To what extent are we nonetheless maritime, I ask non-stop. And why do I write as you ride me? I learned the hard way I mustn't be given fish sauce inside of two years. As if there is something to own. See to it,

§

How sweet was it when we caved-in: you, Lotte Ya, taken with Berryman's bats, digressing, which ironed me, right. Did you get my box of buns? [Two honey three onion five mushroom no raspberry.] Did you hum mid-bite at any point? If so, please send them scores.

Sandy ➡ *Lotte:*

I never expected wings.

Lotte ➡ *Sandy:*

You cannot wave. I get it.

Sandy ➡ *Lotte:*

Why did it take you nearly four pages to say I'm sexy.

§

How *did* you keep your knuckles clean, Lotte, with all that crawling and scurrying and scrambling in Pas De Pepins, amylase opera? Lemon? Brush? Hush? How fast you like your bread? Are you even the one?

   Sandy
   The Bison Lovebird

CODA

Proust died in time

For us all

To be here

Lotte

Hey! Lotte

I to please

I to please

Put all of New Boise's electricity in our no-nam

-e

[fuse]

He knew she lived somewhere near river because he lived on it. Mornings, her hair passed by him on river surface and come evening returned to her. He waited until he knew each strand. Then, having cleaned himself with flour and dressed in red, he walked until he found a brick hut. There was no entrance.

That night, he felt the roughest parts with his fingers, and though he did not find where she exited, the sounds he made pleased him. Second night—by now his reds were fading—he thought as he touched other parts: *My hunger is cilice, dead heat dead shot dead time.* By fifth night, he was doing with his throat what he imagined river would do if it had a throat.

○

By noon next day, he'd taken her strands and hung them in the trees. BOIS would have them. Each time she summoned 4Winds: world was instrumental.

○

In six months, they had three children, whom they named Fanny, Fanny, and Osprey.

So: world was stochastic hijiki.

○

He lifted her onto shale near river to show bird-eating birds what he and she were made of: names. Birds did not need these shale-lovers to function; they did not want shale-lovers to function.

As she brought him to her lips, she made him see through the jade brouillard that had settled in their valley and ruined all trees not marked with fern-ash (CRISP SHOUTOUT TO MORBIER).

It was natural what they did. Even the words. Even the dancing—drenched—away from light.

◯

She tugged on his sleeves of clay. He looked past her, saw two herons colliding, leaving dust on a frog's lower lip. Fusain dropped from pines and said «If either of you desires to move armoire riverside and see what happens—now's the time.» So she forgot what she had wanted to say, he skirted the duties herons had given him, and they went to her Aunt's place to fetch beige armoire, whose name was Fossa. In her Aunt's yard, they picked up three cherry-colored feathers near Pierre De Ronsards. Within a quarter-hour, they'd glued feathers around Fossa's keyhole and left beige Fossa by river that moved so slow.

River did not mind cherries. And river loved armoires, but river could not stand the color beige. So river dived down to the bottom of itself, found mud that could pass for lips, and then river coated armoire with lips.

Fossa, after the thirty minutes she had paid for were up, said «What is it you think you are doing?» River said «You were an orphan. Now your home is my reach. You weren't that attached to your color, were you?»

«Nope» said Fossa.

○

He knew half her body was clay. He just didn't know which half.

He chose a cypress. He chose a noose. He steered himself with gills he'd found near their river-hut. They were shaped like lemons and sat three.

He gave her—when he found her hanging from pine—the cypress. She said «This looks new.» «No» he said. «It's old» he said. «Beige» he said «and circumstantial.»

He offered the noose to 4Winds, who swanned it into residential cream. She saw and said «Now we are talking rosace.»

He cupped BOIS and gave another, Echo, a bath. Echo understood his hut to be cold, which is why she took her bath *outside* his proving ground.

○

«Are those they, my mother's horses?» «My namesake» he continued «died with sunglasses on, and I am blessed to somehow be able to put out fires with beige.»

Echo and she disagreed about Cassiopeia. «What the fuck, Echo?» she said. «I thought everyone knew about fundus» Echo replied and turned into a gray sail and spouted sunflower grease onto her companion's uterus. Her children would lose their arms. Would get muddy playing trumpets.

○

He knew which half. It smelled of lemons.

○

Her face was mostly oval, for once she had touched a bronze feather that had fallen from catalpa and did not throw it back up to its cave of light. He loved that her face was mostly oval. He would rest his face on hers and feel he was swimming in every ocean. And she knew this is what he felt, though he had never told her.

He did not know what had happened beneath catalpa. He loved its effects but he could do nothing when one day he brought her bronze feather and—after she looked at him as though he were some sort of tugboat—she changed into smoke. She changed into wine-colored smoke and left through the windows they had cleaned earlier that morning. She was gone. He went to river for answers. River had nothing for him, not even when he tossed her shadow into it, though river was mildly thankful.

○

He returned to his hills and found his cilice. He hollowed a gourd and drummed for three days. Still—nothing. He returned to river and handed over her hair. River said «I want another like Fossa.» «No» he said, as he steered toward her mountains. He found her on a bridge looking at bathers below in lime-green underwear talking with trout. «What do you want for lunch?» he asked. She did not know. Something flew by and gave a look as if to tell them, though the bridge was made stronger by rust, it hated lime-green.

○

He had not told her that he called where he lived *hills* and where she lived *mountains*. So when they came across a mound of earth with trees of dark mint and tiger-eye, she said «This could be one of my mountains» without knowing that it passed more for one of his hills.

But he was silent. He knew that names keep people, animals, and islands apart, that some islands could eat the same meals from the sea every day and eventually have faces that looked the same.

She took him to where he had been only once before, yet this time, with her warm body and warmer steps beside him, he saw his hills as angelic pubic bones. Then he proposed they build a hut apart from their past, so they could always be ready to call in the horses at a half-closing of eye and shell.

○

She knew he sometimes lived in brambles, for brambles were sweet and available to anything with hands or a half-good idea. At dawn, he blushed and she—more often than not—was able to siphon it into river that passed beneath her house mostly made of nettles.

She waited until she knew each junction, then she packed her shears and made for field. A second dawn was upon them by the time she arrived—beady, undressed, singing—her shears doing the lights.

○

She waited for him in her mountains. He waited for her in his hills. Sadly, beigebeige butterflies blinded them before they knew the way to the other.

Confiscate their wings. Or not.

○

«In just an hour, she had my feet in ruins.» «He took my hair and tied it between the trees. He said this would make the world instrumental. I said, we'll see won't we?»

Beigebeige called their cousins, but their cousins were too busy chewing through cloture de fer to answer questions about Guido and his infinite patience. Their whole lives they had wanted to be clay—they also desired mold of August sea-winds—and they made Guido suffer their desire.

○

The hills walked all over the mountains. The lovers touched like hooves: *look past lordosis into lordosis.* The swans were quiet, too.

○

Colline was still barking at cypresses at 9 a.m. It was not air that made her. Not air that made her do this. He still did not understand what *chair* meant. Out of respect to stillborn dawn, he placed an eucalyptus eye by each body of water he loved.

○

When he took off his feathers, he could breathe better, but—since breathing and flying had become nearly one in recent months—his breathing fell to frags. For she was in her mountains and he was defrocked in his hills.

He had brought it upon himself: licking canvasses clean. The look of their faces as he finished a Chagall! Not that he particularly liked Chagall; his works just tasted good, and you cannot argue with taste. He had licked half the world's paintings to know what others dreamed, and he was tired of not breathing, so he found his peach and beige feathers (They went on first.) He put them on and hummed «Alaska ain't so FAQ.»

Then he put on his wine-colored ones and managed to play *Doctor Gradus ad Parnassum* with only three mistakes, yet each was met with a cry from the earth. We should clarify: a cry from his hills. Not bad for a bird-eating bird, he thought, as he left his pine to mirror beigebeige who darts through air as if it were gospel free of additives.

○

She tested edges of nature for love and dye, and she failed: «Shit, just where is my tiara?»

The tiara was gone. It had fused into his pine. He would never fly again.

Pine is pine, but pine is giant's idea of closure.

○

«I am on to how you turn pines inside-out to benefit the sky» he said. «What are you suggesting?» she said. «Just look at that one» he said, «how you left saliva on the lowest branches, how it's still a little yellow from all the air passing through it.» «I don't see anything» she said.

«I never want to go on another bridge in my life» she said. She blamed bridge for him saying that sometimes she was like the strands. He was not planning on going anywhere soon.

○

She held the back of his neck and part of his left cheek with her right hand and the back of his hand and part of his left temple with her left hand. His eyes like a Boar's showed through and told her that she needed to take him to his river, that they had remained too long in her triangle of pines, and that he might no longer be able to dance.

So she made him stand while she put on his hide, and then they followed the source to where the river was fifty feet wide. «Yes» he said. «Thank you.» «But where is my crane?» he asked. «I thought you said it would still be here when I returned. I need it to make room.»

She pointed to river, and he saw that it had rust in its teeth and dust on its cheeks. «I believe» she said «river is telling you that it will provide what you need, that you should not look elsewhere, except toward me.»

«May I have a cup?»

○

He watched as alabaster rain covered one of his hills. One of his cranes was now the center of things. I wish I were holed up with you, he thought, instead of my rose water and chair. But then the hill returned. She called and said «Sesame, let's go see river tonight at 8 p.m. Then we can catch the last of the swans.»

A friend of both of theirs met them at river with a candle on each shoulder. «I learned this at culinary school» he said. They left him after a half-hour to his fires, after they had seen his necklace torn off by waters and after they had seen the swans.

They were the last of the swans because river was changing.

No veins no game.

O

Finally, he knew she lived in the mountains because he lived in the hills. Every morning he watched as her lips marched down like an unemployed clown. Then he put on his clay trousers, beamed, touched his hens, put the plaster away, and shushed angels: can they even be loud?

She came at him with a scythe made of his interpretations, then she came at him as a stream of broken deities. He stopped her with optics from LALA and then resumed rebuilding the area's pines from the waist down. He wanted her to know his hills. Her mountains grinned. The peace cries had begun.

She knew he was something for the kids. He knew she was SUSTAIN.

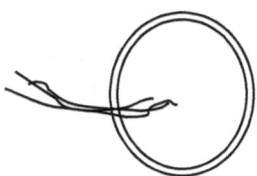

○

Snapdragons fastened to his forehead were one sign that things were going well but strait-laced. He had found her looking down a seventy-three meter well, half her hair gone—but on the left side of her skull he saw a sundial ribbon. And after she had shown him how halfway down a quartz beam jutted out, they left for her house in the mountains.

It was on their walk there that the snapdragons must have come to reside on his head—blue ones, rust ones. She said when they arrived that she liked them as part of his head, that they went well with her sundial complex. He agreed without thinking. They took a bath.

The ribbon disappeared, the blue ones disappeared. Someone knocked. They did not move except to pick up a candle that had fallen over. They relit it.

○

He waited for her call, which he thought would come in part from the triangle on her left cheek. While he waited, he watered the only two plants he could find. He listened to pickaxes working in the street below that sometimes sounded like sleigh bells and wished she would sleigh on over to his room and give him the other cheek for his eye. A turquoise trade.

The windows were curtained with the hieroglyphic for frozen waterfall, which reminded him to treat her to another bath when she visited. He had left his hills to live in a city room because he thought there would be more flowers to choose from. He also needed new forms of sweetness.

What are they picking at, he thought, as he touched air around him. He saw a flake of something at eye level, which was eighty feet above the street, and felt like crying all over again. And what *has* that girl just dropped from her window—failed sunflower seeds, three cushions for ants, five kidney beans?

○

She told everyone she knew she knew—for a fact—that he loved to circle any word that began with *sol*. He did not mind. The worst that ever happened was that he lost the right to use birch branches for a week on his body. He recovered by taking her into the forest and making her fetch a square inch of bark from every tree. She did not mind; she knew they were for a large skin.

Skin was to tell of diaspora and continuity of moss on everyone's eyelids.

She cleaned his tongue with her tongue and said «Today we go to your hills, sweet shingle shiner.» He had once climbed up onto the school roof to moderate a discussion between arriving rain and departing frost. He had rolled off the roof and fell into lilacs. Since then, she had called him «sweet shingle shiner.» She loved lilacs, too, and even kept a photograph of Lilac of the Year 1985 on her refrigerator.

They went to his hills. He said «But these are not your mountains.» She said «I know, but I thought you could show me where you dive into the earth.» «Oh» he said. «There, there, and there. Any questions?» «Let us go to my mountains» she said and took him by the ears because they both had discovered they liked that game.

It was sky's ahem.

Acknowledgments:

Thanks to editors at *Bombay Gin, Mud Luscious, Timber,* and *typo* for publishing portions of this manuscript.

Thanks to the Literary Arts MFA program at Brown University for providing time, $, and ethereal space in which to begin this project.

Thanks to Opo Books & Objects for listening to a sleepless pitch on a plane. And also for peerless production.

Thanks, finally, to Gabrielle Lucille Fuentes: I'd never have finished this book without your goodness and grace.

www.ingramcontent.com/pod-product-compliance
Lightning Source LLC
Chambersburg PA
CBHW020619300426
44113CB00007B/705